Skydiver

Saving the Fastest Bird in the World

Celia Godkin

pajamapress

It is spring. High in the sky, a peregrine falcon heads north. She flies on and on, until she spots a familiar cliff face. This is her nesting site, where she returns year after year. She descends and lands gently on a rocky ledge near the top.

The peregrine waits patiently for her mate to join her. When her sharp eyes spot his familiar shape, she lets out a welcome cry: *"Witchew, witchew."*

Wanting to impress the female with his mastery of the skies, the male greets her with a spectacular aerial display. First he flies high in the sky. Then, with breathtaking speed, he plummets toward the earth. No animal on earth travels faster than a diving peregrine.

At the bottom of his dive, he sweeps upward in an exuberant loop-de-loop. The female sees that her mate had lost none of his hunting skills. Joyfully she rises up to join him.

Together, they swoop and tumble in a dazzling courtship dance.

Over the next few days, the female peregrine lays four eggs. They rest in a shallow depression the pair has scraped out on the ledge. While the large female guards the eggs from predators, the smaller male hunts for both of them.

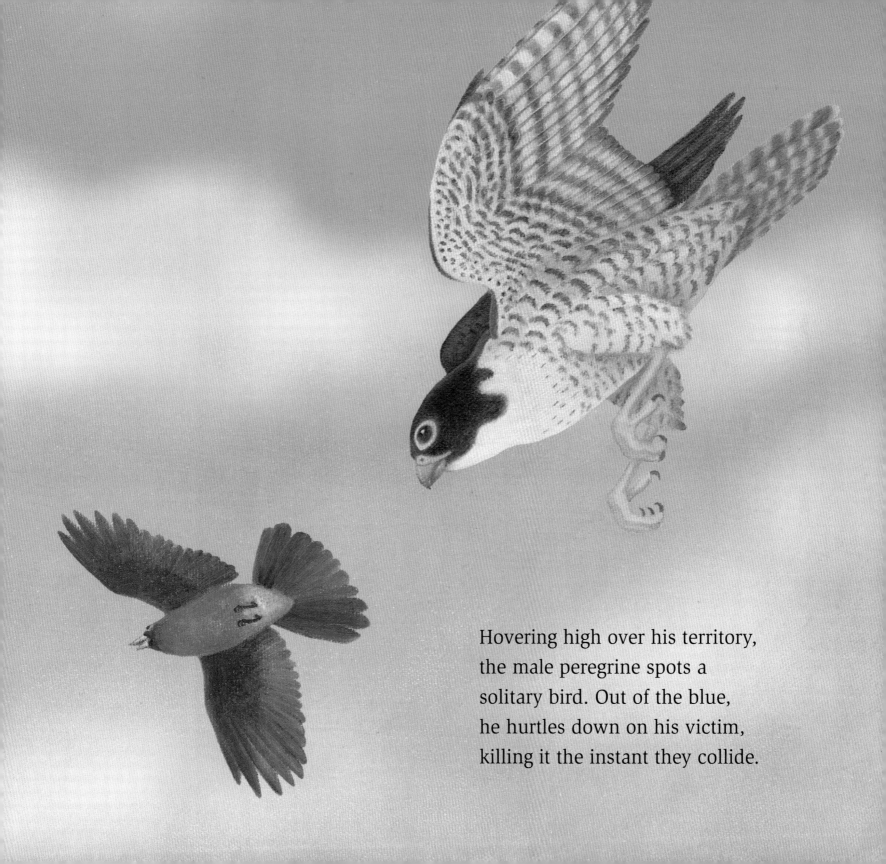

Hovering high over his territory,
the male peregrine spots a
solitary bird. Out of the blue,
he hurtles down on his victim,
killing it the instant they collide.

As the male peregrine carries his prize back to the
nest, he spots two people near the top of the cliff.
One of them is lowering herself on a rope over the
edge. The female peregrine cries out in alarm: "*Cack
cack cack cack,*" and flies off to escape the intruder.

The woman moves carefully down the rock face
until she is within reach of the eggs. Then, one by
one, she places them gently in a special pack that is
strapped to her body. With the eggs safely stowed,
she winches herself back up to the top of the cliff.

Long after the humans have disappeared, the peregrines fly around and around, shrieking in distress: *"Cack cack cack cack."*

A week or two later, the female has laid another three eggs. She is guarding them from intruders when her mate flies down to the nest, carrying a bird he has just killed. As the female takes the food and settles back on her eggs, she hears a faint crack. Two of the eggs have broken under the combined weight of the mother and her food.

The peregrines will raise only one chick themselves this year…but their first clutch of eggs will be raised by humans.

All over the land, birds were in trouble. For the
past quarter century, small aircraft had sprayed
farmers' fields with a pesticide called DDT.

DDT killed many harmful insects, but it also
accumulated in the bodies of insect-eating birds.
Birds of prey like the peregrine falcon, which ate
the insect-eating birds, accumulated the most
DDT of all.

DDT didn't kill birds of prey, but it made their
eggshells so thin they broke easily. Many were
unable to raise any chicks at all.

When people discovered what DDT had done to wildlife, a great protest movement began. Led by scientists and conservationists, ordinary people came together to fight for animal rights and the health of the environment. They succeeded in getting DDT banned.

In the years following the ban on DDT, many bird populations began to recover. The peregrine falcon, however, had disappeared from great tracts of its former territory. To save this spectacular flyer—the fastest bird in the world—people had to make a special effort.

Bird experts and volunteers from all walks of life came from across the continent to help save this magnificent bird. One of them was the young woman who scaled the cliff to take that first clutch of eggs.

The falcon rescue teams know that peregrines often lay a second clutch if the first is destroyed. They hope the birds will raise more chicks.

The team takes the eggs to a sanctuary and places them in an incubator. In this warm, protected place, the fragile eggs have a better chance to survive. Sure enough, three weeks later, four downy chicks hatch into a strange new world.

One of the four hatchlings will be kept at the sanctuary and hand fed by her human captors.

When she is two years old, she will be paired with a captive male from a different nest. Over the years, in the safety of the sanctuary, she and her mate will raise brood after brood of chicks.

Some of her chicks will remain in captivity. Others will be released into the wild.

The other three hatchlings are kept from human contact so they won't become tame. They are fed through a hole in their nest box. After a few weeks, they are moved to a nest platform on the side of a cliff, where their food will be delivered through a tube that runs down the rock face.

Early one morning, as the sky is lightening in the
east, a great horned owl is flying home to roost.

When a sleepy chick stirs in the nest, the owl's
sharp eyes spot the movement. Silently, she
sweeps down and plucks the chick from his perch.

The volunteer who feeds the chicks is saddened to discover that one of his nestlings has vanished in the night. He knows a great horned owl has most likely carried it off. There's a good chance the predator will return.

The volunteer calls the sanctuary staff. They decide to move the remaining two chicks to the city, where there are no great horned owls.

The chicks are placed on a ledge, high up on a skyscraper. They are fed dead pigeons, which are dropped down a feeding tube. Soon the volunteers observe the young falcons swooping and diving on live pigeons as they learn to hunt for themselves.

One of the two peregrines claims the skyscraper ledge for herself. She finds a mate and, in time, they raise a family of their own.

Her brother flies off in search of a mate. Perhaps he will return to the countryside to live wild and free. Perhaps he will stay in the city.

In spite of the many setbacks encountered by the peregrines and their human helpers, the peregrine rescue effort has been a success. Peregrine falcons can be seen once again soaring and diving in the skies, not only over their traditional wild territories, but in cities too.

Look up! Maybe there's one living near you.

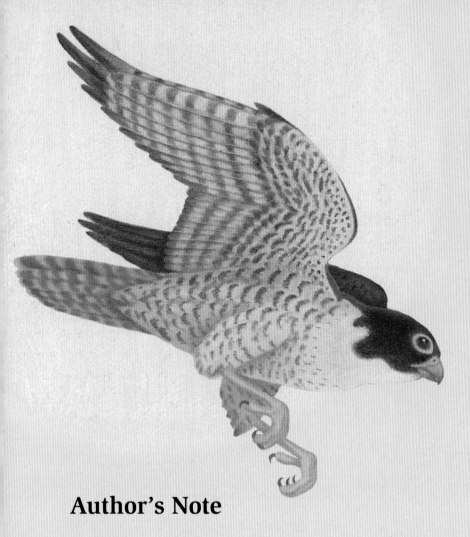

Author's Note

How fast is the fastest bird in the world? The top recorded speed for a peregrine falcon in a power dive is 242 miles (389 kilometers) an hour. To watch a peregrine in flight go to **earthsky.org/earth/fastest-bird**.

Birds like the peregrine falcon have been instrumental in raising awareness of environmental problems, especially those caused by the use of pesticides such as DDT (dichloro-diphenyl-trichoroethane). Many people date the modern environmental movement from the publication in 1962 of Rachel Carson's ground-breaking book *Silent Spring*, which described the negative impact of DDT on wildlife, especially birds.

Developed in the 1940s, DDT is a pesticide that was used increasingly in the 1950s and 60s to control insect pests that attack crops and livestock as well as those that carry human diseases, such as the malaria mosquito. Once injested, DDT can't be eliminated and, as a result, it becomes more concentrated in animals higher up the food chain. DDT interferes with birds' ability to make eggshells. Birds of prey like the peregrine are the most affected because they're at the top of the food chain.

Silent Spring spurred thousands of concerned citizens to rally in demonstrations protesting the use of DDT. The book was heavily attacked by the pesticide industry, but its scientific foundation stood the test of time and DDT was banned for most uses in Canada in 1969. The US followed suit in 1972.

Though the peregrine falcon lives on every continent except Antarctica, it is not abundant anywhere. DDT had a devastating effect on peregrines everywhere it was used. By the 1960s no breeding pairs were found east of the Rockies in the United States. Canadian populations were also struggling.

The recovery of the peregrine in North America was due largely to two programs begun in the 1970s: the Peregrine Fund at Cornell University in Ithaca, New York, and the Canadian Wildlife Service in Alberta. Their work centered on breeding peregrines in captivity and releasing them into the wild.

When the breeding programs realized that many of the fledglings they released to nest sites in the wild were being lost to predators, they tried placing the birds in nest sites on high buildings in cities where there are no great horned owls or eagles. With plenty of small birds for them to prey on, the peregrines adapted well to city life.

Some city nest sites are equipped with cameras, which means the birds can be closely monitored and their progress can be shared with the public. Enter **peregrine falcon webcam live** in your search engine to watch peregrines raising their young via one of these cameras.

The peregrine rescue efforts were so successful that the U.S. Fish and Wildlife Service removed the peregrine from its list of endangered species in 1998. The Committee on the Status of Endangered Wildlife in Canada listed peregrines as endangered in 1978, downgraded this to threatened in 2000, and, in 2017, decided they are no longer at risk (with the exception of some populations in British Columbia that are still of special concern).

As peregrines recovered, government funding of rescue efforts was withdrawn. The peregrine fund (**peregrinefund. org)** is now a publicly funded charity that works to protect the many raptor species worldwide that are under threat from a new array of pesticides, habitat destruction, and global warming.

For more information and extension activities about peregrine falcons and DDT, download the free *Skydiver* teaching guide at **pajamapress.ca/skydiverteachingguide**

The author would like to thank Marcel A. Gahbauer of McGill University for his invaluable assistance in checking the scientific accuracy of this book. The Raptors in Duncan, B.C., provided a direct encounter with a wide variety of birds of prey, including peregrine falcons.

This revised paperback edition first published in Canada and the United States in 2020
First published in hardcover the United States and Canada in 2014
Text and illustration copyright © 2014 Celia Godkin
This edition copyright © 2020 Pajama Press Inc.

10 9 8 7 6 5 4 3 2 1

www.pajamapress.ca   info@pajamapress.ca

Canada Council   Conseil des arts
for the Arts   du Canada

ONTARIO ARTS COUNCIL
CONSEIL DES ARTS DE L'ONTARIO
an Ontario government agency
un organisme du gouvernement de l'Ontario

Canadä

The publisher gratefully acknowledges the support of the Canada Council for the Arts and the Ontario Arts Council for its publishing program. We acknowledge the financial support of the Government of Canada through the Canada Book Fund (CBF) for our publishing activities.

Library and Archives Canada Cataloguing in Publication

Godkin, Celia, author   Skydiver : saving the fastest bird in the world / Celia Godkin.
ISBN 978-1-927485-61-3 (bound) .--978-1-77278-186-1 (pbk.)

    1. Peregrine falcon--Juvenile literature. 2. Endangered species-- Juvenile literature. I. Title.
QL696.F34G63 2014   j598.9'6   C2013-908350-2

Publisher Cataloging-in-Publication Data (U.S.)

Godkin, Celia.
    Skydiver : saving the fastest bird in the world / Celia Godkin.
[32] pages : col. ill. ; cm.
Summary: The story of a peregrine falcon and its mate's struggle to raise their young is told against the backdrop of scientists' efforts to understand the raptors' decline in the wild. After a devastating effect on the bird's lifecycle is linked to the pesticide DDT, the world's fastest bird must depend on humans to recover and thrive once more.
ISBN-13: 978-1-927485-61-3
ISBN-13: 978-1-77278-186-1 (pbk.)
1. Peregrine falcon – Behavior – Juvenile literature. 2. Peregrine falcon – Ecology – Juvenile literature. I. Title.
598.96 dc23   QL696.F34G634 2014

Manufactured by Qualibre Inc./Print Plus
Printed in China

Pajama Press Inc.
181 Carlaw Ave. Suite 251 Toronto, ON M4M 2S1

Distributed in the US by Ingram Publisher Services
1 Ingram Blvd. La Vergne, TN 37086, USA

This book is for the new clutch:
Joshua, Ethan, Noelle, Tariq,
and Sophia